METALLICA
EASY GUITAR WITH LESSONS
VOLUME 1

T0057165

Also available: Metallica Easy Guitar with Lessons, Volume 2 (02500419)

ISBN 978-0-89524-923-4

Visit our website at www.cherrylane.com

INTRODUCTION

This book is for the less experienced player who wants to play the music of Metallica. Obviously, without guidance, it would be difficult for anyone just starting out on guitar to play this material. Therefore, we have created these arrangements for the player who seeks exciting, accurate, and challenging music, but who is more comfortable with this simpler format.

Presented here are off-the-record chord voicings and licks, along with introductory lessons for each song. The more difficult solos are not included, but can be found in the more advanced books on Metallica's music from Cherry Lane's Play-It-Like-It-Is series.

Keep Rockin',

The Editors

CONTENTS

Arranged by Steve Gorenberg and Kerry O'Brien
Cover photography by Ross Halfin

THE FOUR HORSEMEN

Lesson

This high-energy single-note riff doesn't get hairy until bar 4, when you have to change strings and execute hammer-ons. The hammers are all spaced a quarter note apart, so at least there's no tricky syncopation to deal with.

Triplets can be tough nuts to crack, because they don't necessarily fall into the convenient right-hand picking pattern of down-up-down-up. That's the case here, plus you have to switch strings in the process! If that doesn't throw you, try staying in time when the rhythms switch to straight eighths (use a metronome or drum machine to test yourself). Fortunately, the tempo is a manageable ♩=102.

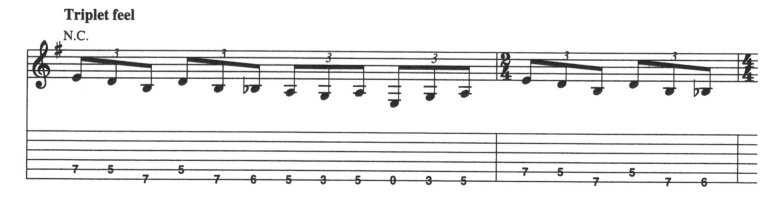

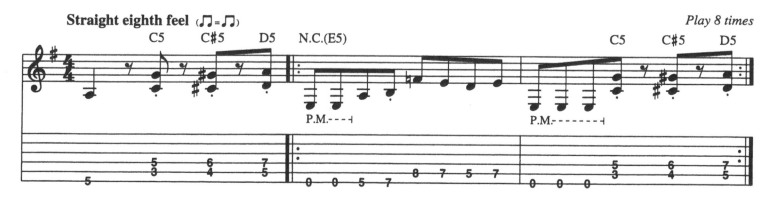

The Four Horsemen

Words and Music by
James Hetfield, Lars Ulrich
and Dave Mustaine

4

They've come to take your life.

On through the dead of night with the Four Horse-men ride

or choose your fate and die!

Oh, yeah, yeah!

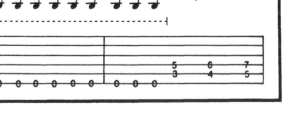

Additional Lyrics

2. You've been dying since the day you've been born.
   You know it's all been planned.
   The quartet of deliverance rides.
   A sinner once, a sinner twice,
   No need for confession now.
   'Cause now you've got the fight of your life. *(To Chorus)*

3. So gather round young warriors now
   And saddle up your steeds.
   Killing scores with demon swords.
   Now is the death of doers of wrong.
   Swing the judgment hammer down.
   Safely inside armor, blood, guts and sweat. *(To Chorus)*

SEEK & DESTROY

You'll be tempted to perform the figure on beats 2 and 4 as a hammer-pull, instead of just a hammer. Don't. Instead, work on sneaking an upstroke on the note immediately following the hammered note. The last measure contains only notes from the E blues scale (E G A B♭ B D).

Two beats down, two beats up is how your right hand plays this next figure. In bar 1, beats 3 and 4 (the two beats up) are *dyads*, or two-note chords. Notice that the roots are on top (compare the dyads to the chord symbols above), and the fifth degree of the chord is on the bottom. This is known as an *inversion.* Again, we have five of six notes from the blues scale in the descending single-note passage.

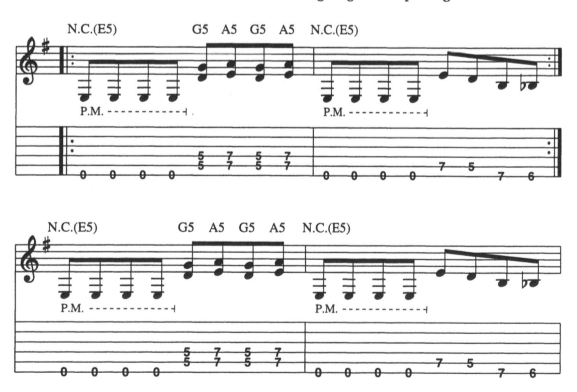

Seek & Destroy

Words and Music by
James Hetfield and Lars Ulrich

1. Scan - ning the scene__ in the cit - y to - night. We're look - ing for you__ to start up a fight.
2.3. *See additional lyrics*

There's an e - vil feel - ing in our__ brains,__ but it's noth - ing new. You know it drives us in - sane.__

Additional Lyrics

2. There is no escape and that's for sure.
   This is the end we won't take anymore.
   Say goodbye to the world you live in.
   You've always been taking, but now you're giving. *(To Pre-chorus)*

3. Our brains are on fire with the feeling to kill.
   And it won't go away until our dreams are fulfilled,
   There is only one thing on our minds.
   Don't try running away 'cause you're the one we will find. *(To Pre-chorus)*

FOR WHOM THE BELL TOLLS

If you place your left-hand 3rd finger (the ring finger) on the 5th-string B in beat 1, you'll have an easier time playing this two-bar power-chord figure. You won't have to change fingers for any subsequent chords, and you can keep your hand in roughly the same, fixed position.

Rhythm Figure 2 goes to a triplet feel with this "Dragnet" motif. The presence of $B\flat5$ and F5 give the passage Locrian (in E: E F G A $B\flat$ C D) leanings.

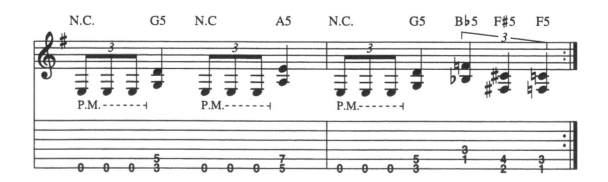

10

Riff A is a one-bar figure repeated eight times. Maintain strict alternate pickng (down-up-down, up-down-up) even though the triplets and irregular string crossings will conspire to confuse you. Be sure to observe the palm-mute indication in between the staves. Retaining a palm mute while your right hand crosses strings requires some practice.

This one-bar fill is in the Dorian mode (in E: E F♯ G A B C♯ D), which means it has a chromatically raised sixth (indicated by the C♯). This fill is similar to the one above, except that the palm mute begins on beat 2.

For Whom The Bell Tolls

Words and Music by
James Hetfield, Lars Ulrich
and Cliff Burton

FADE TO BLACK

Here's a gentle, loose, arpeggiated accompaniment played on acoustic guitar. Let all notes ring as long as possible, and work for even articulations on every note.

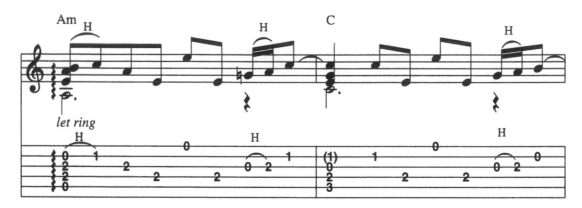

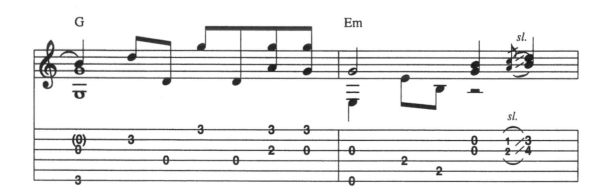

A slow-moving single-line comprises the eight-bar melody. Here are the last four bars, where you have to put bends on half the notes. The vibratos on the half note and dotted half note could also be considered bends of sorts, so your left hand is really wiggling in this section. Begin the passage with your left-hand 3rd finger on the 12th-fret and slide up to the 14th fret on the 3rd string.

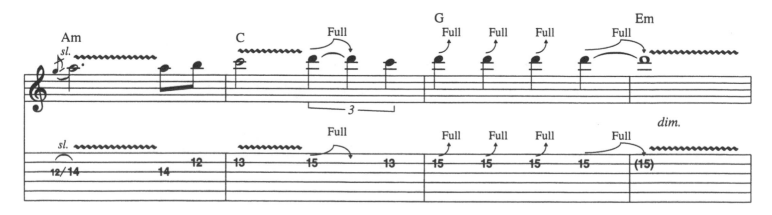

Fade To Black

Words and Music by
James Hetfield, Lars Ulrich,
Cliff Burton and Kirk Hammett

15

CREEPING DEATH

The tempo here is quite fast (♩=184), so to grasp the syncopated effect first in your mind, think of the pattern as 3+3+2 for each bar. This is your textbook metal riff right here, as played by masters James and Kirk.

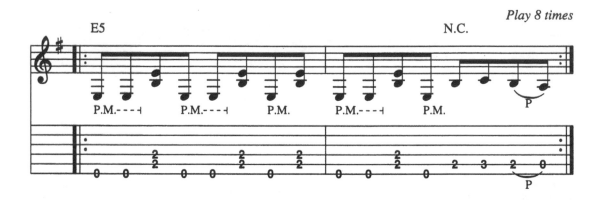

Towards the end of the song, another figure with a 3+3+2 scheme appears. This time it's more obvious because the last note of the first and third bars is tied to a dotted half note. This gives the mind (both the listener's and the player's) a chance to absorb the rhythm pattern that has come before.

Creeping Death

Words and Music by
James Hetfield, Lars Ulrich,
Cliff Burton and Kirk Hammett

1. Slaves, He - brews born to serve to the phar - aoh.
2.3. *See additional lyrics*

Heed to his ev - 'ry word, live in fear.

Faith of the un - known one, the de - liv - 'rer.

Additional Lyrics

2. Now, let my people go, land of Goshen.
Go, I will be with thee, bush of fire.
Blood running red and strong down the Nile.
Plague. Darkness three days long, hail to fire. *(To Chorus)*

3. I rule the midnight air, the destroyer.
Born. I shall soon be there, deadly mass.
I creep the steps and floor, final darkness.
Blood. Lamb's blood, painted door, I shall pass. *(To Chorus)*

MASTER OF PUPPETS

Lesson

There are a couple of tricky techniques in the opening riff of this Metallica classic. Notice in bar 2 the first power-chord slide is from an upbeat to a downbeat (1½ to 2), but that in the second half of the bar the two eighth-note slides both begin on a downbeat and slide to upbeats. Taken slowly, it may not seem that difficult, but once you get up to performance tempo (♩=220) you begin to rely more on feel, so whether a technique begins on the beat or off the beat makes more of a difference.

The 5/8 bar should be counted as 3+2 (say "1 2 3 1 2"). A good way to lead up to this is to count the preceding bar not in quarter notes but as two groups of four eighth notes ("1 2 3 4 1 2 3 4"). So the *counting change* actually comes between bars 2 and 3, even though the meter weirdness is between bars 4 and 5.

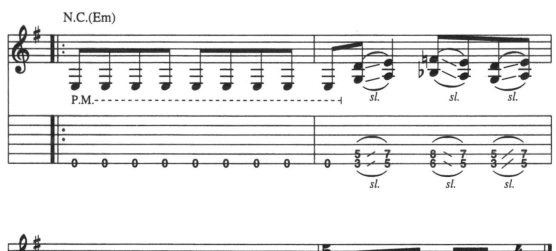

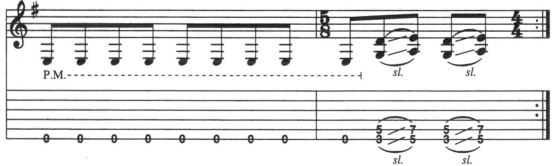

Relief comes in the form of the next riff, which has no tricky syncopation to speak of, nor any meter changes. The D# in bar 4 does lend a bit of harmonic strangeness to the figure.

Master Of Puppets

Words and Music by
James Hetfield, Lars Ulrich,
Kirk Hammett and Cliff Burton

23

ded - i - cat - ed to___
I will run_through you, __

how I'm kill - ing you. ____
now I rule_ you too. ____

(Half time feel)
Pre-chorus

Come crawl - ing

fast - er, _____

o - bey your mas - ter, _____

your life burns fast - er. _____

O -

bey your ___ mas - ter, mas - ter. Mas - ter of Pu - pets, I'm

Slower ♩ = 110

Rhy. Fig. 3

(end Rhy. Fig. 3)

E5   F#5 G5 F#5   G5   F#5 G5 F#5   G5

P.M.----------------   P.M.----------------

w/Rhy. Fig. 3 (2 times)

F#5   G5 F#5   G5   F#5   G5 F#5   G5   F#5   G5 F#5   G5

Mas - ter,   mas - ter,   where's the dreams that I've been af - ter?   Mas - ter,   mas - ter,

F#5   G5 F#5   G5   F#5   G5 F#5   G5   F#5   G5 F#5   G5

prom - ised   on - ly   lies.   Laugh - ter,   laugh - ter,   all I   hear, or   see   is   laugh - ter.

F#5   G5 F#5   G5   F#5   G5 F#5   G5

Laugh - ter,   laugh - ter,   laugh-ing   at   my   cries.

Double time ♩ = 220

D.S. al Coda

G   F#

pick sl.
(steady gliss.)

sl.

sl.

Coda

N.C.(Em)

P.M.----------------   sl.   sl.   sl.   P.M.--------------

sl.   sl.   sl.

(w/Laughter)

E5

Play 4 times

Ha!   Ha!   Ha!   Ha!

sl.   sl.   sl.   sl.   sl.

sl.   s.   sl.   sl.   sl.

WELCOME HOME (SANITARIUM)

Lesson

Things seem simple enough for the first bar and a half of this riff. Each ascending arpeggio stretches across four strings; the pattern fits well in the 4/4 scheme. But at bar 2, beat 3, the pattern goes to a syncopated 3+3+2 scheme, and is complicated by the addition of the grace-note slides. Practice the figure first without the slides, and then try to incorporate them. The tempo is a moderate ♩=98.

At the chorus there comes this devilishly tricky maneuver: 16th-note double-stop slides starting on the off-beats. At bar 2 there's a fast single-note figure that leads off with a slurred 16th-note triplet and ends on the low-E downbeat of bar 3. Notice that except for the little upswing at the last note of the bar, the figure is a descending E minor scale.

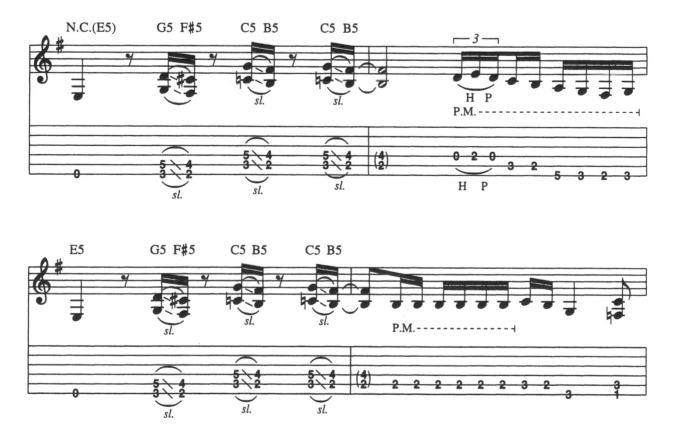

Welcome Home (Sanitarium)

Words and Music by
James Hetfield, Lars Ulrich
and Kirk Hammett

San - i - tar - i - um,

just   leave   me   a - lone.

ONE

Technically, this is perhaps the simplest riff in the book. Let the notes ring languorously out, and don't dampen the open G string in bar 4, which should ring through the entire next bar.

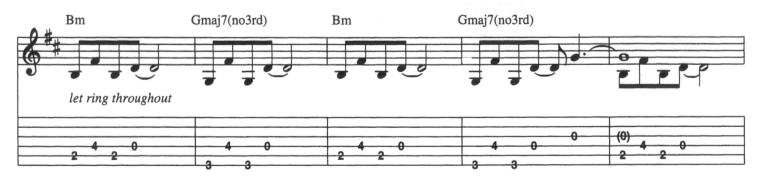

Give this next figure a sort of military, tin-soldier stiffness when you play it. Don't hit the low B's and G's too hard. The tendency is to really thwack them because they're anchor points. If you listen to the recording, though, you'll hear that the articulations between these and the higher notes are pretty even.

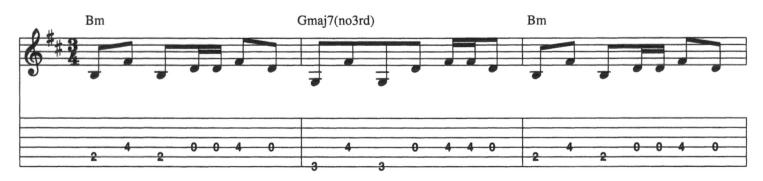

Here's your 16th-note triplet workout. As is typical for this passage, the low-E's are palm muted and the rhythmically longer power chords are accented. Play both eighth notes at bar 2, beat 4 with downstrokes.

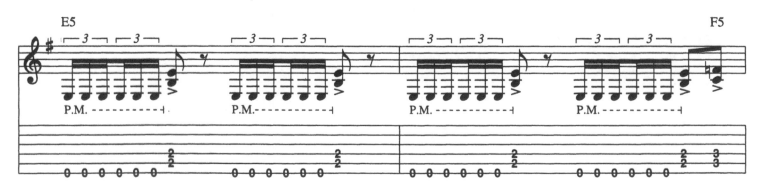

One

Words and Music by
James Hetfield and Lars Ulrich

*Battlefield sound effects for approx. 15 sec.

Hold my breath as I wish for death.___ Oh please God, help me!___

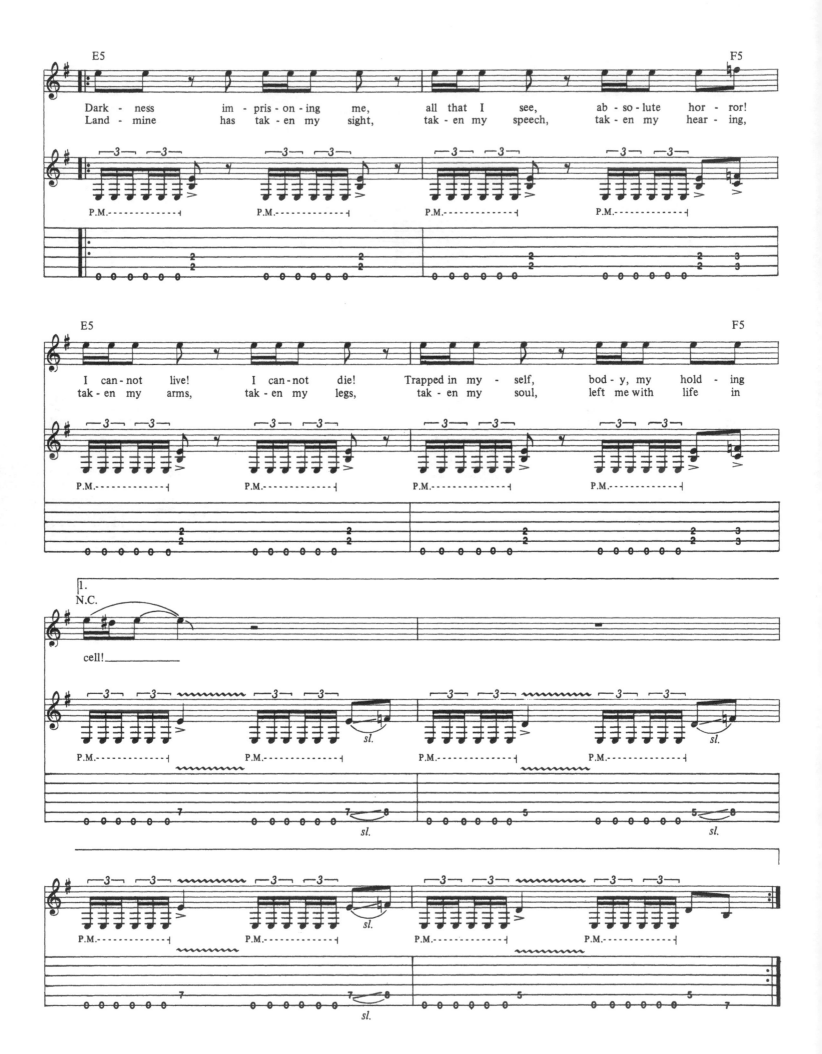

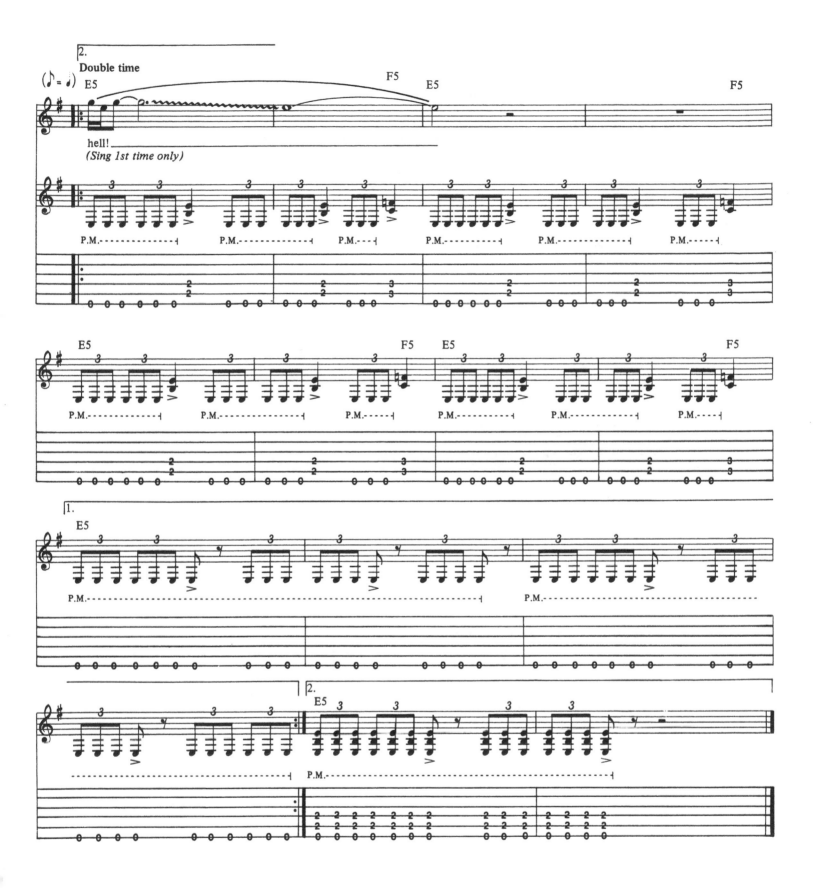

Additional Lyrics

2. Back in the womb it's much too real, in pumps life that I must feel,
But can't look forward to reveal; look to the time when I'll live.
Fed through the tube that sticks in me, just like a wartime novelty;
Tied to machines that make me be. Cut this life off from me!
Hold my breath as I wish for death, *etc.*

HARVESTER OF SORROW

Because of the tie that connects beat 2½ to 3, you may have trouble playing the 16-th note B in perfect rhythm. Practice the figure without the tie; that is, play the E's twice so you get the feeling of the two-16ths-and-an-eighth figure on beat 3. Then put the tie back in (leave the second E silent).

There's a lot of added stuff in this figure. Look first to the right-hand articulations. Almost every note has either an accent or a palm mute attached to it. Then to the matter of the left hand. There are vibratos on the downbeats of each bar. Even though the notes are short (eighth notes), they still get a wiggle from the left hand. The mix of single notes and five-note chords is no picnic either. Practice this one real slow at first.

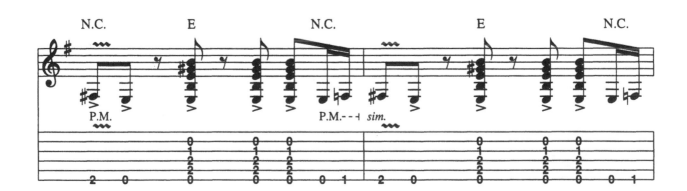

Harvester Of Sorrow

Words and Music by
James Hetfield and Lars Ulrich

*On repeat, Gtr. I strikes E5 chord again at this point.

1st, 2nd Verses

1.My life suf - fo -cates. Plant - ing seeds_ of hate. I've loved, turned_ to hate.
2. *See additional lyrics*

Trapped far be - yond_ my fate._ I give, you take this life that I__ for - sake.

Been cheat -ed of my_ youth. You turned this lie__ to truth._____

Additional Lyrics

2. Pure black looking clear. My work is done soon here.
Try getting back to me. Get back what used to be.
Drink up, shoot in. Let the beatings begin.
Distributor of pain. Your loss becomes my gain. *(To Pre-chorus)*

ENTER SANDMAN

Lesson

This entire song is about eighth-note pickups, so practice giving yourself a *four count* (four beats lead-off) and come in between beat 4 of the count and beat 1 of the music. This two-bar riff has its share of techniques. There's a slide on beat 2, a vibrato on beat 3, a palm mute on beat 4, and then we're back to the pickup to the new measure.

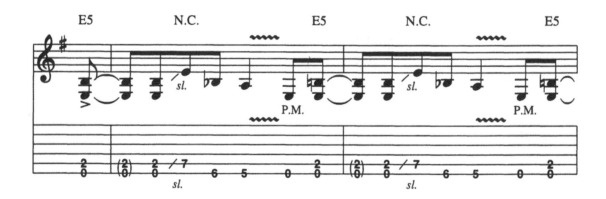

The pre-chorus figure is rhythmically identical to the preceding riff. Notice the unusual placement of the palm-mute indication on beat 1½.

Enter Sandman

Words and Music by
James Hetfield, Lars Ulrich
and Kirk Hammett

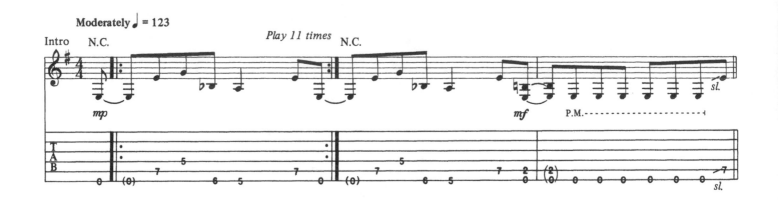

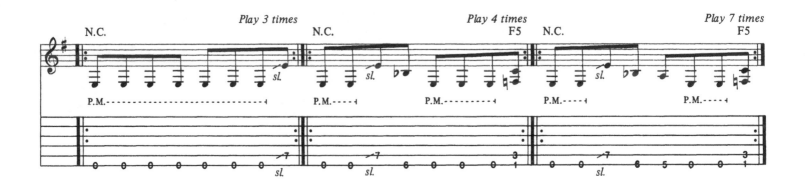

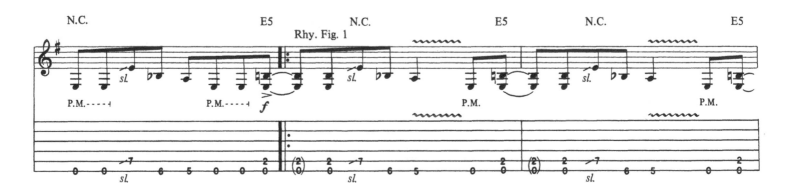

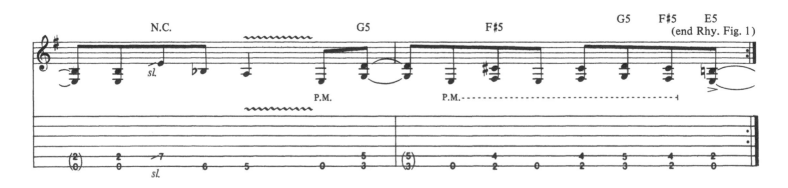

SAD BUT TRUE

The rhythm on beat two, involving a tied 16th note followed by a 16th-note rest, is a lot simpler than it looks. Just let the tied note sound for a short time before damping the sound with your right hand. The desired effect is to have a little blank spot between the tied note and the power chord on beat 2¹/₂. Notice that the single-note line beginning at beat 3½ uses only notes from the E blues scale (E G A B♭ B D).

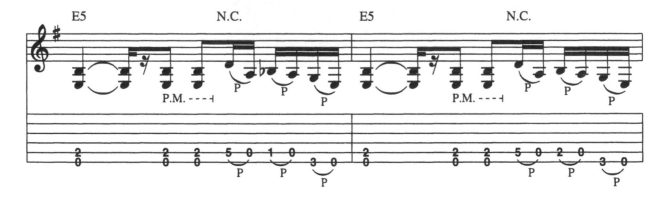

There's a mixed bag of techniques to be found in this next riff. There are palm-muted single notes, palm-muted power chords, accents, eighth-note triplets and gallop figures. The first and second bars are rhythmically identical, and the palm mutes always cross the bar line.

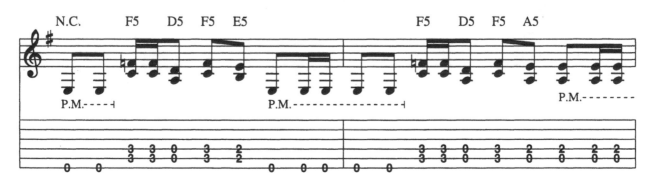

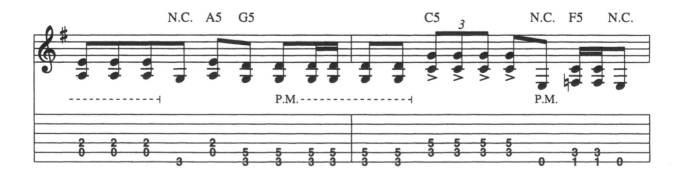

Sad But True

Words and Music by
James Hetfield and Lars Ulrich

WHEREVER I MAY ROAM

Lesson

The first three bars in this opening riff are rhythmically identical, except that there's no trill on bar 2, beat 4. A trill is executed by rapidly hammering and pulling the two notes indicated. Strike the principal note (the larger) first and hammer and pull to and from the note indicated in parentheses.

The Interlude riff starts out like the opening riff, but takes off at bar 2 into parts unknown. For the first two bars every beat has some right- or left-hand technique applied: accents, palm mutes, slides, trills, hammers or vibrato. This makes the passage very intense sounding.

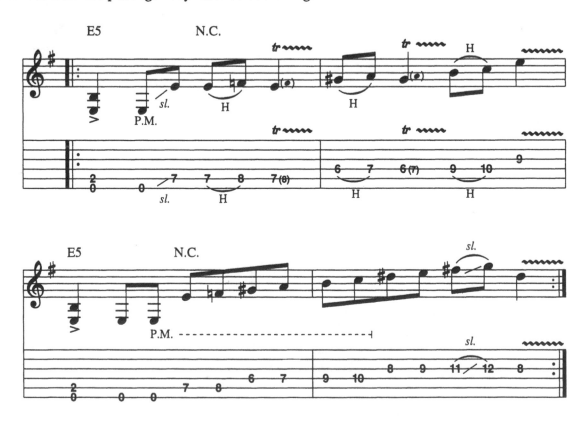

Wherever I May Roam

Words and Music by
James Hetfield and Lars Ulrich

55

NOTHING ELSE MATTERS

Lesson

This is just about the simplest fingerstyle pattern you'll find: all open strings, one finger per string, and the strings played in ascending and descending order. The tempo is a crawling ♩.=46, too.

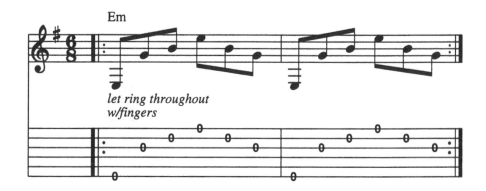

The verse riff is only a little bit harder than the opening riff; rhythmically, the first four notes are the same and the last four are doubled up—played twice as fast. In bar 2, we encounter what is known in fingerstyle terms as a *pinch*—two notes played together with the thumb and ring fingers of the right hand. Notice that your thumb has to play the last two 16th notes of the bar in rapid succession.

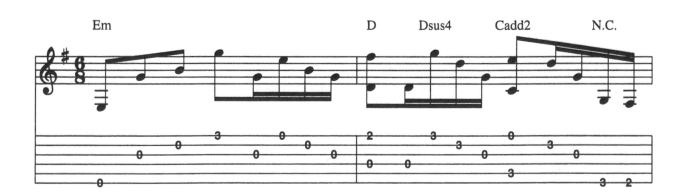

Nothing Else Matters

Words and Music by
James Hetfield and Lars Ulrich

Additional Lyrics

2. Never opened myself this way.
   Life is ours; we live it our way.
   All these words I don't just say.
   And nothing else matters.

4. *Repeat 1st Verse*

5. *Repeat 2nd Verse*

• TABLATURE EXPLANATION/NOTATION LEGEND •

TABLATURE: A six-line staff that graphically represents the guitar fingerboard. By placing a number on the appropriate line, the string and fret of any note can be indicated. For example:

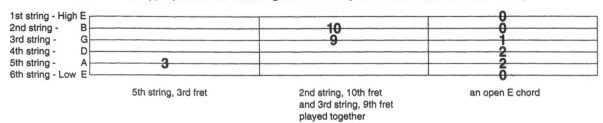

1st string - High E
2nd string - B
3rd string - G
4th string - D
5th string - A
6th string - Low E

5th string, 3rd fret

2nd string, 10th fret
and 3rd string, 9th fret
played together

an open E chord

Definitions for Special Guitar Notation

BEND: Strike the note and bend up ½ step (one fret).

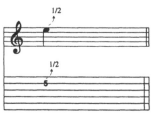

BEND: Strike the note and bend up a whole step (two frets).

BEND AND RELEASE: Strike the note and bend up ½ (or whole) step, then release the bend back to the original note. All three notes are tied; only the first note is struck.

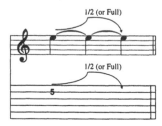

PRE-BEND: Bend the note up ½ (or whole) step, then strike it.

PRE-BEND AND RELEASE: Bend the note up ½ (or whole) step, strike it and release the bend back to the original note.

UNISON BEND: Strike the two notes simultaneously and bend the lower note to the pitch of the higher.

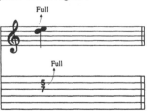

VIBRATO: Vibrate the note by rapidly bending and releasing the string with a left-hand finger.

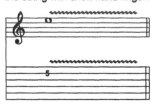

WIDE OR EXAGGERATED VIBRATO: Vibrate the pitch to a greater degree with a left-hand finger or the tremolo bar.

SLIDE: Strike the first note and then with the same left-hand finger move up the string to the second note. The second note is not struck.

SLIDE: Same as above, except the second note is struck.

SLIDE: Slide up to the note indicated from a few frets below.

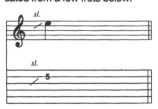

HAMMER-ON: Strike the first (lower) note, then sound the higher note with another finger by fretting it without picking.

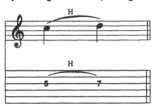

PULL-OFF: Place both fingers on the notes to be sounded. Strike the first (higher) note, then sound the lower note by pulling the finger off the higher note while keeping the lower note fretted.

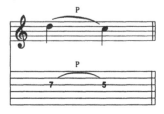

TRILL: Very rapidly alternate between the note indicated and the small note shown in parentheses by hammering on and pulling off.

TAPPING: Hammer ("tap") the fret indicated with the right-hand index or middle finger and pull off to the note fretted by the left hand.

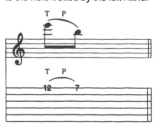

NATURALHARMONIC: With a left-hand finger, lightly touch the string over the fret indicated, then strike it. A chime-like sound is produced.

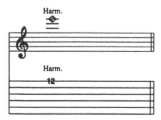

ARTIFICIAL HARMONIC: Fret the note normally and sound the harmonic by adding the right-hand thumb edge or index finger tip to the normal pick attack.

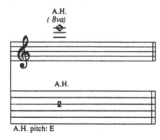

TREMOLO BAR: Drop the note by the number of steps indicated, then return to original pitch.

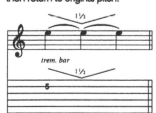

PALM MUTE: With the right hand, partially mute the note by lightly touching the string just before the bridge.

MUFFLED STRINGS: Lay the left hand across the strings without depressing them to the fret-board; strike the strings with the right hand, producing a percussive sound.

PICK SLIDE: Rub the pick edge down the length of the string to produce a scratchy sound.

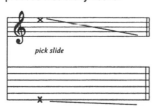

TREMOLO PICKING: Pick the note as rapidly and continuously as possible.

RHYTHM SLASHES: Strum chords in rhythm indicated. Use chord voicings found in the fingering diagrams at the top of the first page of the transcription.

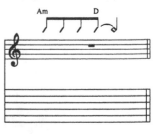

SINGLE-NOTE RHYTHM SLASHES: The circled number above the note name indicates which string to play. When successive notes are played on the same string, only the fret numbers are given.

Definitions of Musical Symbols

8va	•Play an octave higher than written
15ma	•Play two octaves higher than written
loco	•Play as written
pp *(pianissimo)*	•Very soft
p *(piano)*	•Soft
mp *(mezzo-piano)*	•Moderately soft
mf *(mezzo-forte)*	•Moderately loud
f *(forte)*	•Loud
ff *(fortissimo)*	•Very Loud
(accent)	•Accentuate note (play it louder)
(accent)	•Accentuate note with great intensity
(staccato)	•Play note short
	•Repeat previous beat (used for quarter or eighth notes)
	•Repeat previous beat (used for sixteenth notes)
⅟	•Repeat previous measure
‖: :‖	• Repeat measures between repeat signs
‖: 1. 2. :‖	•When a repeated section has different endings, play the first ending only the first time and the second ending only the second time.
D.S. al Coda	•Go back to the sign (%) and play to the measure marked "To Coda," then skip to the section labeled "Coda."
D.C. al Fine	•Go back to the beginning of the song and play until the measue marked "Fine" (end).